CANUTING THE WAVES

JACKIE HARDY

Canuting the Waves

BLOODAXE BOOKS

ISBN: 1 85224 463 1

First published 1998 by
Bloodaxe Books Ltd,
P.O. Box 1SN,
Newcastle upon Tyne NE99 1SN.

Bloodaxe Books Ltd acknowledges
the financial assistance of Northern Arts.

Cover printing by J. Thomson Colour Printers Ltd, Glasgow.

Printed in Great Britain by
Cromwell Press Ltd, Trowbridge, Wiltshire.

For Allan

'I would like to have it explained,' said the Mock Turtle.
'She can't explain it,' hastily said the Gryphon. 'Go on to
the next verse.'

Alice in Wonderland

Acknowledgements

Acknowledgements are due to the editors of the following publications where some of these poems first appeared: *All Lombard St to a China Orange* (The West Press, 1993), *Bare Bones, Blithe Spirit, Evening Chronicle* (Newcastle), *Haiku Quarterly, Haiku Spirit* (Ireland), *Haiku World: An International Poetry Almanack* (Kodansha International, USA, 1996), *Hi* (Japan), *Inkstone* (Canada), *The Iron Book of British Haiku* (Iron Press, 1998), *Keywords, the old moon and so on* (New Zealand Poetry Society, 1994), *Other Poetry, Poetry Marathon '93 Charity Anthology* (Bryan John Allen, 1993), *Poetry Review, Presence, Psychopoetica, Red Herring, What Poets Eat* (Foolscap, 1994) and *Writing Women*.

Contents

Whale-watching on the *Alpha Beta*

This sea-horse is a bucking bronco
in a tidal race. My tranche is ten

to twelve o'clock, a piece of cake
that tilts time back and forth.

In flotsom, my eyes imagine fluke
and fin, each white horse a hurry

of feeding gulls. For hours nothing
bigger than a harbour porpoise,

a colony of common seals. In and out
of islands, the sea frenzies with guillemots;

the air flocks with fulmers, shags
shearwaters, as thick as midges

on the Isle of Mull. The crew bait
me with fishermen's tales, the ones

that got away: yesterday's pod of orca
heading north, the school of dolphins

leaping to a rendezvous, the young minke
who nudged the dinghy while they watched.

Resentment rises like a stream
of diver's bubbles. Then I saw it –

distant, a back, a graceful arc, no more.
'Nine o'clock,' I scream. We wait.

I win the Mars bar dangling from the mast,
seasoned now with spray, a sweetener

for sighting the day's first whale.
Today, the first and last.

Throbbing up the loch, past the cottage
with the bright pink roof, once

the captain's place, I stow memories:
my minke, a Mars bar, a sunburned face.

Cetacean

But who will hear those first notes,
the leitmotif, the song of oestrus,

sounding in her monstrous body,
vibrating through her massive bones?

Who will hear the surge of singing
above the guttural of engines,

falsetto of a thousand voices
cabling over the ocean floor?

If the dredger's thrum disperses,
will he catch her plangent echoes?

Will there be an answering chorus
across the darkness of the blue?

Wet Feet

What do you expect if you are always
King Canuting the waves? You're bound to end
up damp. Why can't you walk foot-stepped bays,
keep in the shadow of cliffs? As a friend
I offer this advice for what it's worth:
build your castles where others have built theirs,
avoid quicksands, give rock-pools a wide berth,
marsh and mudflats may catch you unawares.
Remember, be alert for wind-blown spray.
Walking that lacy line is never safe:
a little sand in your shoes will not weigh
you down, soon you will hardly feel it chafe.
It's no good thinking that your toes are webbed.
Come back! At least wait till the tide has ebbed.

Thirteen Ways of Looking at Tynemouth

I

This place is rock and wind
and water; the river a tidal gash,
a go-between sky and sea.

II

At ebb tide, the rocks;
a man in waders
winkling out shells.

III

Against a force eight
a seagull
labours;
rests;
glides away.

IV

Mist corrodes grey water.
A foghorn follows the silence.

V

At dusk
wraiths hover over
Black Midden rocks;
the cry
of a roosting seabird;
the moon's reflection
floating on the waves.

VI

Behind Collingwood's back
wind frets the Priory ruins
until you'd swear a bell
tolls for compline, matins
vespers.

VII

Outside
the best-kept villa
a rank of wheelchairs.

VIII

Wind surfers scuttle
to and fro
inside pincer piers.
Sails claw a blue sky,
make a sudden dip.

IX

In the car park starlings hustle,
bicker over picnickers' crumbs.
Above the ice-cream van's engine
birdsong, the slap of a pennant.

X

A chill wind –
replacing 'Vacancy' sign
seaside landlady.

XI

On the wind an engine needles.
Locked in a channel the Shields ferry
stitches its way from quay to quay.
In the reeking cabin commmuters huddle;
turn a blind eye to Collingwood's stony glare.

XII

A coin sights two circles
of jaundiced sand,
an idle tanker;
the lighthouse lens,
goes blind.

XIII

The Swedish ferry
passing the lighthouse
a bank of cumulus.

Shell Song

Always the sound of the sea. On summer nights
the lap and plash of waves leached by moonlight;
flopping slowly; lolling through the motions.

The boom and crash of winter storms; ocean
pounding rock, where white flowers of spray fall
to nothing; frail wraiths of sailors who fail

to gain the shore. But most of all, rolling
breakers; rhythm of their music reeling
monotonously across the reaches

of perception; understanding their speech;
the tongue of water. Beached on this arid
shelf, dust muffles faint vibrations hurried

on the wind; littoral voices who lisp
consolation. Strain after their whispers.

Sea Sickness

I must go back to the rail again, to the sea and the lowering sky,
And all I ask is a small hole where I could curl up and die.
The engine's whine, the wind's howl and the white horses bobbing
Add a greenish cast to my grey face, set my poor head throbbing.

I must go back to the rail again, for the call of the rising gorge
Is an urgent call, a real call, that may not be ignored.
And all I ask of the wind today, send the white spew flying
Out to sea, not blown back on my sleeve, solidifying.

I must go back to the rail again, to where the waves and stomachs heave,
And the ship rolls and my eyes roll and the weather brings no reprieve.
And all I ask to give that smug sailor's arse, when we dock in Dover,
One quick kick, then a quiet kip when the long trip's over.

creeping things

snail's signature –
morning sun shining
on the dotted line

in the moonlight
snails dine *à deux*
in the cat's bowl

Computer Aided Design: Creation

In the beginning was the number cruncher.
On the face of it darkness screened.
God had cold feet, terminal-user worry.
He searched the void, put in a warm boot.
God logged on, remembered the colon
and there was light.

Then came the word. And the word was God
was trying to jump before He could run.
Hands on, God pressed space, split-screened heaven
and earth from the waters. At the interface
God inserted disks, backed up the system
with a graphic display.

The package had chips with everything,
so God got bold, accessed the menu in colour;
blocked the earth with green, the seas blue;
entered fish and fowl. With another byte
God updated fields, returned beasts, cattle
and creeping things.

He opened a window, watched them browse.
God saved beasts and cattle, scanned creeping things.
Somehow there were bugs in the system.
God reprocessed data, executed, maximised;
gave creeping things another pair of legs,
a sting in the tail.

Then God created first generation humans
in His own icon. To the female He gave
the second generation function, the womb,
so that she might be fruitful and multiply
even unto the millionth generation.
And He called her Wombman.

Then God copied the female, cut and pasted,
deleted the womb. And the male He called Man.
God scrolled through His works, monitored progress.
God saw that it was good and that His name
was in the hi-scores. Level six ended the session.
God logged off.

Now an omer is the tenth part of an ephah

On Sunday afternoons, scrubbed free of sin,
a portcullis pattern in her palm,
she thought her way round each next corner
mitigating miles to Sunday school.

In the church's thick quiet, her ears
ached for the strangeness of Bible talk.
The hymns tightened her throat,
summoned passions she ought to suppress.

Sometimes the threepenny-bit hung on her palm,
reluctant to drop into the collection.
In her hand the details began to fade.
On the way home she spoke in tongues.

That Certain Age

Our faces map
the routes we've taken.
We count infirmities;
watch to see who's next
and where.

It has its compensations:
accumulated wisdom,
a falling-off the roundabout
of dissipation.
We swing towards a little kindness
to ourselves:
dress appropriately for weather,
do things we like more often.

It has its certainties.
One is death.
Another that my legs
grow more like mother's every day.

Not Now

It won't happen now,
the gasp of admiration, envy,
as an assembly of academics
grasp the sweep, the magnitude
of my intellect.

It won't happen now;
the gold medal,
my face on the immense screen,
the merest smear of tears
for the national anthem,
the raising of the flag.

Seeing strong men
weak at the needs
from the enormity
of my breasts.
It won't happen now.

Now I keep my head out of clouds,
have ambitions
where my head's on the ground:
skipping the tales under ten stone,
my share of slip and tackle,
blotting the pack of the ordinary
and finishing the odd poem.

Keepsake

(i.m. EASA)

That year, while February dragged its heels
in snow, you couldn't wait to see them bloom.

Not peony or rose, your favourite flower
was neither brash nor grand. 'Biennial,'

you'd said, as I watched you plant them up.
Spring sun would find you out, deck-chaired,

your eyes shut tightly, communing with their smell.
Once, I picked you out, among their bright

and simple flowers, filling your damaged lungs
with their strong scent as if it were a salve.

Now, I catch the keepsake of tobacco, sweat,
old corduroys in wallflowers' sweet perfume.

night thoughts

hoping
for shooting stars –
a crick in my neck

feigning sleep –
with each inhalation
the creak of my pillow

all night long
the sound of the waterfall
a remembered dream

Early Warning

A hot-air balloon inspired this sonnet.
Its giant presence came as some surprise.
British Lung Foundation written on it.
Four people dangling level with my eyes.
An uncivilised hour, seven thirty,
for those of us whose curtains are not closed.
What we were at wasn't really dirty,
but people like to do it, unexposed.
Saw the pilot and three old ladies smile;
from my position I could see them well.
Whether courtesy or our lack of style
was the reason I couldn't really tell.
Beware when expressing your affections.
Peeping Toms can come from all directions.

notes from the city

bleak day –
correcting the spelling
   on the beggar's sign

   a tramp sidles by
watching the pavement artist
   draw a crowd

the biggest bumbag
   hung on the woman
     with the biggest bum

Flight-Lieutenant Bigglesworth Sends Algy a Notelet

Sorry you couldn't make Monday.
Ginger and I went to that café
we used to frequent in its heyday.

It's changed. You remember the Bizet?
Well now there's a deejay, no cabaret
and some wild music called reggae.

Guess what Ginger was wearing? Lamé
trousers; his jacket, lilac crochet
and a papier-mâché rose in his toupée.

Naturally, I wasn't so risqué.
I thought we'd agreed to go on to the ballet
but Ginger just had to be outré

and last week, in the theatre foyer,
we met the Wing Commander's fiancée.
I'd like to get under her duvet!

Anyway, Ginger was quite the gourmet.
We ordered. I had the consommé,
he had the pâté. We both had the cassoulet

and the soufflé. He drank gallons of rosé,
I had the usual Dubonnet.
After the coffee Ginger got a faraway

look in his eyes; engaged a waiter in foreplay.
The waiter got sauce down his gilet
and Ginger got brained with some Vouvray.

Before you could say horseplay
Ginger was flat on the parquet.
Hooray I'm au fait with the way

to allay an affray!
The buffet, two tables, an ashtray
entailed a considerable outlay.

Jumped in the coupé and spun Ginger off for an x-ray.
Nothing broken, though I wish he wasn't so blasé.
Now, how are you fixed for a replay, Sunday?

The Essential Guide to Astral Travel

The ultimate in 'get-away-from-it-all',
the seasoned astral traveller will know
any month is suitable for that first
out-of-body experience. Easy to learn,
hovering and soaring can be mastered
with the minimum of fitness. No need
for concern about dietary changes,
nectar and ambrosia are unlikely
to be on the menu, unless you forget
to book that fixed return date flight.
Remember your credit cards; many
a first-timer has been surprised to find
themselves wedged under the ceiling
without money or travellers cheques.
American Express is welcome anywhere.
Insurance is a good idea; in case
of difficulties with the return journey.
Things to look out for –
the fabulous streamlined, high-speed tunnel
with the bright light at the end of it;
reminiscent, according to some travellers,
of that feeling when your children
are about to leave home. Listen for trumpets.
Those of you with acute hearing may catch
the twang of a harp. Don't forget; it's cheap.
And once you've got the hang of it
the universe is your oyster.

Pressing His Suit

He taught me all I know of ironing;
deft hands smoothed my inexperience,
folded my ignorance small as handkerchiefs.

I learned to give trousers that sharp definition,
copied his style with shirts,
weighed his arguments concerning ties, pyjamas.

He impressed me with his talk of steam irons,
how they gave a better finish.
He always finished.

One thing I never picked up –
how to get through the whole pile
without leaving something for another day.

Fridges

What I find mystical about fridges
is their inner light,
their occupation with white space
the hum, click, shake
of their mantra.

My Son and the Long-Eared Bat

Prone it was, night creature on morning grass,
flawless in death. You pulled on rubber gloves
in case of germs, let unfilled fingers pass
across its furry skin as one who loves
or mourns. Noticed ears: long, transparent, veined.
Carefully spread see-through segmented wings
to gauge their span. Noted how they retained
elasticity, hooks to hang to things.
You turned it. Saw its ugly gargoyle face,
wide-open eyes, its mouth a perfect 'O'.
'I think it's great,' was how you put its case,
'Don't you?' Somehow I couldn't answer 'No'.
You claimed, 'It's the best thing I've ever found,'
and gently, with regret, laid it in the ground.

insects

after mosquitoes'
nocturnal whine
starting the new day
from scratch

    reading *al fresco*
an ant steps across
    Bashō's old pond

in the bookstore
two flies settle
    on a romance

Shoot-out at Three Thirty

The kitchen fills with swagger,
saloon bar truculence.
They eye my greeting like an obscene gesture,
reply in groans.

Food humanises them enough
to level at my head
their fully-loaded wants,
half-cocked ideals.

When the stampede slows
they loll in lazy esses,
await the bare-back noes,
then outlaw to music in their rooms.

Bruised, but not blooded,
I polish up my badge,
long for a shot of red-eye
and to ride, alone, into the sunset.

Marriage Lines

At first
we tossed
each other

word for word;
ripples
widening

into sentences.
Muffled
by habit's

dark brown
hood,
I did not

hear
your pensive
rests

becoming
orchestrated
silences;

the words
you failed
to say.

Ring

The profile lost,
the details faded,
it's worn the pattern
of ten thousand days
as smooth as habit.
It knows its place;
a ridge and groove
where skin is softer, pinker;
only aired at night
or when it chafes.
Certainly it's thinner;
sleeves my finger
with a glow from nearer
its eighteen-carat heart;
yet fits tighter every year.

Shift

I was used to her wearing
the thick brown coat of marriage.
It clung about her: twitching
sometimes, tight, shiny, keeping
outside outside, inside in.

When he split, she emerged,
in a sheer soft dress, light as mist,
seemingly a universe of cloth,
her pain rapt in elaborate curls,
floating under the shadow of chiffon.

When she raised her outspread arms,
her sleeves weightless as motes,
I wondered if she might take flight;
exuding from those gorgeous flounces
the reek of vengeance, loathing, fear.

The Difference

I left by the front door
and took the path
less gravelled. By
the love-lies-bleeding
I saw your face
in the window
and for once
we saw eye to eye.
At the weeping willow
I felt the warm yellow
of a smile on my back.

Later I crept
through the back door
to pick up the pieces;
the rest of myself.
There in the kitchen
you were cooking steak, naked.
Nipples hardened by fat spits,
legs freshly shaven,
you seemed to be
rubbing along
the right way.

I asked you
what you thought
you were doing
and could we
get together sometime?
You said
you thought I had split.
And that's how you wanted it.
Your smile
oranged to red
so I split again.

Talking Hands

Through the thick cream of Irish voices
I caught you speaking from across the room.
Your hands hovered like bees making choices
between the promises of gorse or broom.

I pick up your fingered proposition,
the gestured give and take of inference;
watched you wave away the opposition,
signal a line, a pointed preference.

Drawn like water to a lower level,
within the circle of your pantomime,
it seemed cavalier that I should cavil
at the truth of each palmed paradigm.

Out of touch with what you were debating,
led on by the how of your relating.

Self-Portrait with Black Dog

For months it's not around –
chained up
outside someone else's door.

Then the signs –
the howl at dawn,
wet patches at the base of trees
and in the garden, mounds of earth,
the digging up of ancient bones.

After several days
it's slunk inside,
sniffing at my crotch.

When I feel paws
on my shoulders,
the lollop of a long tongue
in my face,
I'm looking for a lead.

Finally
there's nothing for it
but to get out the car,
bundle it into the back,
head for distant moors,
and let it run.

Monday

summer sunrise
familiar shadows
    – longer

spotted
on the the laundry basket
nine ladybirds

on the washing line
shirts semaphore
    an east wind

Witchcraft for Beginners

Today we have charming of warts. Last week
we had cauldron cleaning. And next Wednesday
we shall have what to do before flying. But today,
today, we have charming of warts. Mandragora, germander
and laurel, found in all of the neighbouring health stores,
        are needed for charming of warts.

This is the recipe for wart charm. And this
the incantation intoned whilst steeping the laurel.
And these the ingredients whose names you will know
when you get more familiar. Remember, most branches
of pet shops will have discounts available
        when you get your familiar.

Each of you must have her own order of passes,
which must be kept secret. Please do not let me
see anyone overlooking her neighbour. Conjure the order
of passes by means of this simple mnemonic. Beware
of abusing the power of the lore and spell out
        anyone overlooking her neighbour.

There are discounts available when overlooking
your neighbour, whose name you will know
when you get more familiar. Remember germander,
whilst steeping the laurel. Spell out mandragora
by means of this simple mnemonic and keep secret
        that today we had charming of warts.

Marigold Peace's Mellow Willow Lullaby

The most beautiful words have all the fun
in any language. They murmur silken prose
and dream on golden patios in the sun.

Poets whisper them in lines that pun,
echo in our sleep. Poets love those
most beautiful words. They have all the fun.

Found in tranquil autumn, gossamer spun;
mist; the late blossom of a velvet rose;
they dream on golden patios in the sun.

But crystal winter has them on the run.
Darling dusk, beloved twilight never froze.
The most beautiful words have all the fun.

Caress their mellifluous tones, one by one.
Open with harmony, a melody to close.
Dream on. Silver patios shimmer in the sun.

Sorrow fades when laughter dawns on anyone.
Champagne works magic. Everybody knows
the most beautiful words have all the fun.
They dream on golden patios in the sun.

Botrytis Can Be Troublesome

What was it
about women
that reminded Ruskin
of lilies and rosies?

Was it their delicate beauty,
their purity,
their sweet scent
that dizzied his senses?

Or was it death;
a waxy pallor
raised in stiffling air;
crossed and seeded?

Or braving the thorns;
the training;
taming for the optimum size,
the perfect shape?

Or was it the bed,
fertilised and weeded;
burning unmanageable growth;
the blood and bone?

for all seasons

across a blue sky
the vapour trail fades
faster than it's laid

first day of summer
putting clocks forward
dandelions

light from the bonfire
shining in a child's eyes
miniature fireworks

Christmas morning –
the child with the bike
watches the rain

41

Dora Takes the Stand

Okay.
I admit it.
I opened it.
But how was I to know?

Nah.
I had no idea.
How should I?
It was just a vase
with a Bloomingdale's label on it.
When I shook it
whatever was in there rolled around;
sounded liquid.
I though it was liquor or something.

Well, hell, no.
It wasn't my idea.
What do you take me for?
I'm just a dumb blonde.
It was him.
Always taunting me.
Saying I got feet of clay.

Him? Theo.
My husband.
Always daring me to do things.
Like that time in Central Park...

I guess he got it from Prom.
My brother-in-law.
A guy always do-gooding.
Well he was, till he got
that infection.
In his liver.
Seemed to clear up right enough,
then next day it broke right out again.
Had those medics beat
that's for sure.

Anyhow how can you keep
that kinda stuff in a vase?
Bottled passion?
Sounds like some kinda cheap perfume
to me.
How can you put
old age, sickness, insanity
in a jar?
I ask ya?
I don't see how
you can lock away
them kinda things.
I can't see how
it can be my fault.
Gee, Judge, it really ain't fair
to pin it all on me.

Off the Wall

That geezer Belshazzer had been for a nightcap
and it had turned into a heavy session.
The next morning I awoke to the aroma
of metaphor, smudges on the walls. Here, a clump
of greens: emerald, viridian, sage and olive.
Over there, the browns: chocolate, raw sienna,
burnt umber and a medium rare Vandyke.
After breakfast the colours were joined by assorted
nouns. Later verbs, adjectives, prepositions.
They were behind the wallpaper, seemingly.
You could braille them just as if some manic
letter writer trapped between the mould-resistant
adhesive and the pink Laura Ashley tulips
had graduated to words and was posting them
into my box room. Then they began to phrase themselves.
Troped together they belayed a pitch
up the overhang of the 'T' fall, until
at the summit I noticed full-blown haiku
hanging thicker than petals on the cherry trees
in a Kyotō spring. Limericks followed.
When serious syllabics surfaced I began
to read them off the walls. On the floor
piles of feet shuffled in front of my broom:
the great iambs, trochees, that metrical terror
dactyls. But I should have put them out.
By afternoon they were climbing the walls,
lining themselves up. This time there were regular
stanzas, dirty ballads, slogans demanding
'Free Verse'. At the sight of all that language
the landlord lapsed into cliché. The wallpaper
rep blamed the recycling process. Said the batch
number indicated manufacture from waste
paper from Huddersfield. Finally, I got in
a publisher. 'Are these yours?' he scathed,
looking them over. His words bullied imperceptible
witherings. The past fell away first, began
to fester. There was no future. The present

hung on for several days. At last, parcelled,
neatly labelled, I put them out for collection.
Caught a bin man rummaging through the presents.
'Just looking for something for the wife's birthday,'
he said. He took away 'perfumes', 'dresses', 'rings'.

Sergeant Cowing Remembers 1916

Captain Snowball didn't stand a hope in hell:
oppressed by shells, he snailed towards me,
inch by inch
until, against the odds, he lay beside me
in the crater
carved out by an eighteen-pounder.

Strange, I couldn't feel a thing below the knees.
Not even as he unwound mud-smeared puttees,
roll by roll.
I didn't recognise the legs as mine; the bones
showed white
through blood-smeared skin.

Captain Snowball packed the wounds as best he could.
His last words: 'That one's a Blighty'. We lay
side by side
until the shelling died. Then he raised the stakes;
drew one shot
courtesy of Jerry sniper.

He threw up his hands; fell across me dead.
That night we were dealt each other's company
face to face.
I had no power to move him. For a while he warmed me;
later,
kept off the frost.

The Salmon to the Salmon Fisher
(for Seamus Heaney)

Eager eye set downstream, you wait
    Patiently; the sentence at your desk
    Broken by the offer of rod, bait
And memory of sport and gathering dusk.

And I lie by the bank, resting.
    The river flowing over me refracts
    Green waders, black body flittering
Fisher-made hooks clothed in feather.

I twitch tail, fan fin, the lure
    Quickens your heart and ripples pass
    Between us, tell of an ancient lore
Angling for my body, gutted, behind glass.

Fast streamlines my shape; a sudden
    Whoosh and chevron flight tempts me to bite,
    Chance a gullet full of steel, hidden
In the cunning dip and hue of bait.

Relinquish your rod, return to your lines,
    I spurn your fly as I did Walton's worm.
    Quench your thirst on fisherman's lies,
I swim onward, fulfilling destiny to spawn.

pigeons...

sun up –
the clatter of pigeon's wings
      into the mist

    first light –
  a pigeon struts
on the empty street

buds breaking
on the sycamore
a wood pigeon preens

a twig here and there
the pigeon pair make good
    last year's nest

withered fields –
among rows of garden greens
a flock of pigeons

only when it lands –
  city pigeon
  with one leg

hot chestnut vendor
looking out for the law
    serves a pigeon

    pigeons advance:
with an outstretched hand,
    the toddler retreats

  in the gutter
    a dead pigeon
– the dove-grey of it!

from the pigeon loft
  a solitary cooing
    so low, so low

racked by a cough
stroking his favourite bird,
    the pigeon fancier

    pigeon race –
    suddenly the whistle
    of a thousand wings

the sun's last rays
    two pigeons on the fence
        fluff up their feathers

and other birds

startled in tall grass
the pheasant's wing-beat
faster than my heart

    morning exercise –
    blackbird on the lawn
stretches a worm

cracking snail shells
a thrush leaves empties
    on the doorstep

Broad Beans

come in their own-grown, right-sized Jiffy bags:
long green-padded pods, some straight, some curly.
Like fisted knuckles in thick winter gloves,
subtle undulations hint they're on the pulse;
full of beans. Inside, nestling in white fur,
places marked like cutlery in velvet,
they lie kidney-shaped and flat; their colour,
a green so pale, so seedy, evoking
seasick faces lined up against the rail.
When taken from their suede interior,
yellow attachments puntuate the pod
like commas in an adjectival list.
Cooked, they wrinkle like an uptight scrotum:
assume a pallor, greyish-mauve, dead lips.

The Wife Speaks

Hate and anger had died to an ember
when he came home. He always seemed normal;
perfectly normal. I can't remember
once thinking otherwise. He was warm all
the time to me; never cold. But anger
and hate must have been there, like a dull glow
waiting to grow white-hot; coloured danger
for any woman. Why? How could I know?
They tell me he murdered thirteen women;
did things the newspapers dared not report.
Mutilated them and left them swimming
in blood. Yes, I'm glad he was caught.
I thought I knew him. But deep down, inside,
he was someone else. Someone he could hide.

doubt

hangs around

dries
the edges
of talk

breezes through
the draught-proofing
of company

rattles
the hatches
of meetings

loosens
the guy ropes
of relationships

whistles
up the trouser leg
of blood

making sense

across the meadow
   wind ripples the grasses
      warm breath on her neck

summer's first rose
   inhaling the bouquet
      of his sweat

sea spray
   veiling the cliff
      salt's tang on her lips

from a glass vase
   a fall of wisteria
      low sound in her throat

spring dawn –
   his withdrawing member
      still glistening

Not Waving

Her hands moved like seaweed over rocks
on his cooling skin. She had found him

lying in sunlight flickering through water;
hauled him over the threshold of the surface

back to air. She worked at his chest,
more certain each moment he would never feel

her fingers. When a serpent of sea water
broke from his mouth, she enclosed his lips

with her lips; gave him her breath;
stole the pleasure of his tongue.

One more time, she said, as her mouth moved
down his body, licking the salt on his skin.

In Harrison's Cave

Time ticks off drips
until a million million
mass a micron thick of lime:
slow growths whose shapes
invite a noun.

A stalactite mimes 'The Chandelier',
a stalagmite 'The Frog'.

By a lake
an American tourist presses
a piece of paper in my hand:
a tract that asks
'Is Jesus Christ your Lord
And Saviour?'

Streams weave their egress
through the rock.

God moves in calcareous ways.

Druridge

At dusk the bay becomes itself again.
    Shadows cool the backs of afternoons.
Grey-lag geese take off for roosting places.
    Trippers traipse to cars beyond the dunes.

Marram rustles in an off-shore current.
    Waves make over footprints in the sand.
The city's golden dome backdrops the distance.
    A prick or two of light defines the land.

The sea unmasks a phosphorescence;
    a mist of light surfacing the spray.
Evening grades the bay from grey to blackness,
    erases the encroachments of the day.

Castlerigg

The coldtime has been deep and long.
After each dark I have marked the stone.
It wants but two sets to the planting.

The elders question my tally;
watch for the birds that dip and glide;
keen for the sun's warmth; ignore the moon.

Soon we will trek to the circle.
Our craftsmen will barter the axes
chipped by coldtime firelight for pots, skins.

Our wise men will line up the light
on the stones; calculate the planting.
They will pass over my diligence.

After the prayer and feasting
they will trade me for another.
My man will say nothing. It is the way.

Double Take

She would have known him. Even coffin spruce,
his beard brushed up around the parted mouth.
That dark mole rooted on the concave cheek
he liked to nuzzle in a grandchild's neck.
The lilac lips that she had once kissed back,
lips that whispered nothing, she half-recalled.

She would have known him. Even white-frock purged,
his character brushed-up propriety.
Those dark moods rooted in their private past
whose legacy glints in their grandchild's eyes.
Lips famous for their tales, like fishermen's,
their truths encrusted with each new telling.

Paying Through the Nose

When he told her scent was aphrodisiac
she cruised the Faubourg's parfumeries,
breathed Guerlain, Givenchy, Guy Laroche,
numbered Chanel against each pulse.
She learned to map a convoluted route
across her skin. He nosed each trail
with slow deliberation, until bloodhounded,
no perfume masked the essence of her musk.

When she caught him sniffing around
she fumed; a phoenix that seethed and spat.
Midday found her on the boulevard –
the poissonier, a kilo of his freshest prawns;
the vintner dusted off his stock from Reims.
She lazed towards his flat in tainted heat;
the concierge raised eyebrows at the proffered Krug;
accepted both – the champagne and her missing purse.

She heard he'd hired a coterie of cleaners,
brought new bedding, cushions, carpet, curtains;
aired services to fumigate and exorcise
when neither orris, woodruff nor sandalwood
could muffle the wafted backdrop to his scenes
of love; when he could not trace the high seclusion
of her déjeuner, the cocktail of oaths and prawns
she'd stuffed inside his hollow curtain pole.

She watched from the bar across the street
the day he moved away. She raised a glass
when certain that he meant to take the pole,
a brazen reminder of her fragrant gift.

Objection Overruled

Not only the rape
but the tone of the questions.
Not only the rape
but the latent suggestions.

Not only the rape
but the media's mileage.
Not only the rape
the psychological damage.

Not only the rape
but the hints of temptation.
Not only the rape
but the judge's summation.

Not only the rape
but the lack of repentence.
Not only the rape
but the length of the sentence.

Not only the rape.

Flutter

It shadows grey on grey about her house
and will not look her in the eye.

She listens as she lies in wait for dawn.
It stalks the postman with a stealthy pad.

Mid-morning, she turns her hand to chores;
feels it creep across her tight-strung skin.

At noon it's crunching tiny bones,
leaves emerald stomachs at her door.

Caught napping in the afternoons,
it is the Sphinx of windowsills.

At dusk it throws on camouflage.
She draws curtains, thin, against the moon.

In the dark it's on the prowl.
It calls. Her gut response, the answer.

Chosen

The night is heavy
with the silence
of the temple bell.
As light as the shadow
of a cloud,
the monk's spirit passes.

The woman asks for water
but the bucket has frozen.
The father-to-be brings yak's milk;
hesitates as her body strains,
adjusts the skins.
She asks for water.

At the stream,
in a sudden rush of moonlight,
he cracks icicles from the rock.
The clouds recover the moon;
across the windswept plateau
the tolling of Tashilunpo's bell.

In the tent,
the child slips from the woman
on a tide of blood.
The new mother asks for water
and he offers an icicle.

In her sleep she smiles
into the face of her sleeping son.
She dreams the blurt of the conch,
the shore of Lhamoi Lhatso
and the men divining the waters.

The Blessed Field

She woke to birdsong.
The chack-chack, chack-chack of a dun fledgling
she could not name in Greek nor English.
She watched motes rise and fall in sunlight
lasered through the weave of canvas; breathed
its fevered breath, the prick of mildew, must,
a blossom of wax.

Outside, cool air;
too early, yet, for the thick-hot curtain
that swept away her unity; released
the languid being she'd discovered here,
living beneath her darkening skin.
The one who knew the tongue of ouzo,
the scent of wild thyme.

Through daisies, barefoot;
borage, poppies, convolvulus; her legs
wet with dew, sticky with sap, dusted
with the pollen of a thousand flowers;
towards the red and white of oleander,
whose leather leaves hedged a boundary
above a rush of rock.

At sea a blurt of wind
pouted the sail of a solitary caique.
She held her breath until the gust nimbussed
her hair, then sucking its rawness,
seasoned her lungs. Behind her it moved on,
waved the flowers and grasses of the field,
punished the tent flap.

She turned to the sound
of a bell. On the dusty hillside goats
stretched among the almonds, olives, carobs.
In the village a donkey megaphoned
the start of work. On their way to church
two old women stared past her waved greeting,
ignored her smile.

She found he still slept
when her eyes grew used to the tent's gloom.
She snaked beside him, inhaling the smell
of his sleeping body, lodged herself
to the accommodation of his back.
Stirred at the touch of her feet, he licked
salt spray from the hairs on her arms.